FACT or FICTION?

DO MERMAIDS EXIST?

PETER FINN

Gareth Stevens PUBLISHING

Please visit our website, www.garethstevens.com. For a free color catalog of all our high-quality books, call toll free 1-800-542-2595 or fax 1-877-542-2596.

Library of Congress Cataloging-in-Publication Data

Names: Finn, Peter, 1978- author.
Title: Do mermaids exist? / Peter Finn.
Description: New York : Gareth Stevens Publishing, [2023] | Series: Fact or fiction? | Includes index.
Identifiers: LCCN 2021057041 (print) | LCCN 2021057042 (ebook) | ISBN 9781538280812 (library binding) | ISBN 9781538280799 (paperback) | ISBN 9781538280805 (set) | ISBN 9781538280829 (ebook)
Subjects: LCSH: Mermaids–Juvenile literature. | Ocean–Folklore–Juvenile literature.
Classification: LCC GR910 .F56 2023 (print) | LCC GR910 (ebook) | DDC 398.21–dc23/eng/20211214
LC record available at https://lccn.loc.gov/2021057041
LC ebook record available at https://lccn.loc.gov/2021057042

First Edition

Published in 2023 by
Gareth Stevens Publishing
29 E. 21st Street
New York, NY 10010

Designer: Sheryl Kober
Editor: Therese Shea

Photo credits: Cover (top) and p. 1 Kasa_s/Shutterstock.com; Cover and p. 1 (middle glitter texture) Ron Dale/Shutterstock.com; Cover (bottom) and pp. 1-32 (background texture) Olga Pedan/Shutterstock.com; pp. 2-32 (background texture) Iuliia Tarabanova/Shutterstock.com; p. 3 kattalinks/Shutterstock.com; p. 4 Artinblackink/Shutterstock.com; p. 5 (top) C Salisbury/Shutterstock.com; p. 5 (bottom) Shalyapina/Shutterstock.com; p. 6 New Africa/Shutterstock.com; p. 7 (top) SCPRO/ Shutterstock.com; p. 7 (middle) Katarina Marsalekova/Shutterstock.com; p.7 (bottom) Dancestrokes/Shutterstock.com; p. 8 Barashkova Natalia/Shutterstock.com; p. 9 Obsidian Fantasy Studio/Shutterstock.com; p. 10 (coin) https://en.wikipedia.org/wiki/Atargatis#/media/File:Derketo.jpg; p. 10 (illustration) https://en.wikipedia.org/wiki/Atargatis#/media/File:Kircher_oedipus_aegyptiacus_28_derceto.png; p. 11 https://en.wikipedia.org/wiki/Siren_(mythology)#/media/File:WATERHOUSE_-_Ulises_y_las_Sirenas_(National_Gallery_of_Victoria,_Melbourne,_1891._%C3%93leo_sobre_lienzo,_100.6_x_202_cm).jpg; p. 11 (bottom) Erosha/Shutterstock.com; p. 12 Idea Trader/Shutterstock.com; p. 13 Nick Fox/Shutterstock.com; p. 14 olrat/Shutterstock.com; p. 15 Eroshka/Shutterstock.com; Alexey Pevnev/Shutterstock.com; p. 16 (top) Laura Dts/Shutterstock.com; p. 16 (bottom) Liliya Butenko Shutterstock.com; p. 17 (top) Oleskalashnik/Shutterstock.com; p. 17 (middle) Atelier Sommerland/Shutterstock.com; p. 17 (bottom) Andrea Izzotti/Shutterstock.com; p. 19 Morphart Creation/Shutterstock.com; p. 20 Marzufello/Shutterstock.com; p. 21 Eva Bidiuk/Shutterstock.com; p. 22 Nadya Dobrynia/Shutterstock.com; p. 23 S-F/Shutterstock.com; p. 25 (top) https://en.wikipedia.org/wiki/Fiji_mermaid#/media/File:Feejee_mermaid.jpg; p. 25 (middle) https://commons.wikimedia.org/wiki/File:Feejee_Mermaid_1.jpg; p. 25 (bottom) https://en.wikipedia.org/wiki/Fiji_mermaid#/media/File:Feejee_Mermaid,_shown_in_P.T._Barnum's_American_Museum,_1842,_as_leased_from_Moses_Kimball_of_the_Boston_Museum,_papier-mache_-_Peabody_Museum,_Harvard_University_-_DSC06154.jpg; p. 26 Leonard Zhukovsky/Shutterstock.com; p. 27 (top & bottom) FashionStock.com/Shutterstock.com; p. 28 Nadya Dobrynia/Shutterstock.com; p. 29 (top) Impola Tonatua S A O/Shutterstock.com; p. 29 (bottom) Ari Wid/Shutterstock.com

Printed in the United States of America

CPSIA compliance information: Batch #CSGS23: For further information contact Gareth Stevens, New York, New York, at 1-800-542-2595.

Contents

Words in the glossary appear in **bold** type the first time they are used in the text.

Watching the Water

For thousands of years, sailors have watched the ocean from the decks of their ships. Sometimes, creatures from below the water appear at the surface. Fish and dolphins leap alongside the ship. Whales come up from the depths to breathe. In the past, sailors worried about sea monsters emerging from the deep too. Stories about mysterious beasts were part of sailor folklore, so they watched the water, wondering and worrying.

Some sailors claimed to see something else quite surprising in the water: humanlike creatures! These weren't other sailors who had jumped overboard. They had upper bodies like humans, but instead of legs, they had long, scaly fish tails. Sailors told many tales about these astonishing creatures. They called them mermaids and mermen.

EARLY MAPS

Many early maps weren't created for sailors, but for wealthy people as art. Cartographers, or mapmakers, sometimes included odd creatures, like sea monsters, as decorations on these maps. Some of the weird animals were described in what were considered to be science books of that time. They were often like actual animals but with a strange twist. By the end of the 1600s, as knowledge of the oceans increased, fewer images of imaginary sea creatures appeared on maps.

Early cartographers drew sea monsters and mermaids in the oceans on their maps.

IT'S A FACT!

"Mer-" is a prefix that means "sea." "Maid" is a word for an unmarried, often young, woman.

More to the Stories

Many sailors reported that mermaids swam to the surface and laid on rocks, like some kinds of sea creatures do. Mermaids were described in stories as admiring their reflections, combing their long hair, or wearing shells or pearls. Some looked like people with tails, while others were totally covered with fish scales. They were beautiful or ugly. Some were said to have green or blue skin.

Tales of mermaids and mermen—sometimes called merfolk or merpeople—weren't only about the creatures themselves. Storytellers told of magnificent underwater kingdoms in which these merfolk lived. And, of course, no **technology** existed hundreds of years ago to disprove the presence of underwater people or underwater buildings in the deepest parts of the ocean.

MERMAID PEARLS

Pearls are beautiful gems found inside **mollusks**, including clams, oysters, and mussels. In ancient Japanese folklore, a mermaid's tears created pearls. We now know pearls are formed when outside matter makes its way into a mollusk's shell and irritates, or bothers, it in some way. The mollusk covers the matter with a shiny material called nacre, starting the formation of a pearl. As the mollusk adds layers of nacre, the pearl grows in size.

A mermaid figurehead on a ship's prow, or front, was believed to be good luck.

IT'S A FACT!

Seals and sea lions are two kinds of ocean animals that crawl up on rocks to sun themselves.

The Magic of Mermaids

In many stories, mermaids have special powers. Sometimes they use magic to help people. They grant wishes, for example. Some tell people what will happen in the future.

Other mermaid tales are more frightening. They tell of mermaids that **hypnotize** sailors into jumping into the water and following them below the waves. Some lore says mermaids use song to lure unsuspecting sailors to their deaths.

Just seeing a mermaid could be a bad omen, or sign, of deadly storms at sea. According to a **Norse** text from the 1200s, a mermaid near Greenland tossed a fish toward a ship as an omen that sailors would die in a storm. She'd toss it away from the ship if all would live.

YAWKYAWKS

Aboriginal peoples of Australia describe water spirits that live in streams and tide pools. Sometimes they're called *yawkyawks*, which means "young women" in the Kunwinjku/Kunwok language. But the Kuninjku people may call them *ngalberddjenj*, meaning "the young woman who has a tail like a fish." Besides fish tails, these spirits can have long green hair, like strings of algae. They may walk on land at night or even fly. They bring the water people need, but can also cause storms if angered.

This is a modern artist's idea of what a mermaid might look like in her seabed home.

IT'S A FACT!

In the *Ramayana*, an Indian epic, the mermaid princess Suvannamaccha aids the hero Hanuman. She is still a figure of good luck in Southeast Asia.

Ancient Mermaids

The oldest recorded legend of a mermaid may have come from the ancient region called Assyria. This myth of Atargatis dates back to around 1000 BCE. According to the tale, Atargatis was a goddess who fell in love with a shepherd, whom she accidentally killed. In grief, she threw herself into the sea. But other gods saved her by turning her bottom half into a fish tail. Atargatis (shown above) became a sea goddess—and a mermaid.

The Babylonian god Oannes, a merman, was first written about around 300 BCE. According to some myths, Oannes had the body of a fish but also a human's head and feet. He swam to the shore to teach humankind about writing and other arts.

SIRENS' DEADLY SONGS

Sirens of ancient Greek myth were half woman and half bird. They, like mermaids, were once blamed for shipwrecks. Sirens' beautiful but deadly songs **enchanted** sailors. According to some tales, the songs forced sailors to steer off course and wreck their ships against rocks. In the Greek epic called the *Odyssey*, written between 725 and 675 BCE, the hero Odysseus fills his brave crew's ears with wax to escape the sirens' song.

In the *Odyssey*, Odysseus wished to hear the sirens' deadly song. He asked his crew to tie him to the ship's mast before they passed the creatures.

IT'S A FACT!

Babylonia and Assyria are the names of empires that were located in ancient Mesopotamia, an area that's part of today's Iraq.

Merfolk Around the World

Merfolk stories come from all over the world. Besides tales of sirens, ancient Greeks told stories of gods who could live in the water. Triton, a merman, was the son of Poseidon, the god of the sea. Triton lived with his parents at the bottom of the ocean. He carried a large seashell, which he blew to make waves or calm them. He could create dangerous storms on the ocean with it.

The Inuit people of Canada and Greenland tell the story of Sedna. In one account, she was tossed from a boat by her father. Her fingers became whales, seals, fish, and other sea creatures. She sank to the bottom of the ocean where she continued to live as a goddess and watch over the animals she created.

SELKIE LORE

Some claim the Irish and Scottish told tales of mermaids called merrows, or *murúcha*. However, these folktales are more modern and seem to have come from Germanic or **Scandinavian** lore. This includes the tales of the Selkies, who appear as seals in the water but can take off their skins and walk on land as humans. If Selkies lose their skins, they cannot turn back into seals and return to their watery homes.

This statue of a Selkie can be found in Denmark's Faroe Islands, between Iceland and Norway.

IT'S A FACT!

In African folklore, Mami Wata is a water spirit often shown in mermaid form. She can heal the sick and bring good luck, but she also drowns those who anger her.

The Mermaid of Warsaw

Mermaids are depicted, or shown, all over the city of Warsaw, Poland, including as statues, carvings, and other decorations. In fact, a mermaid has long been a part of the city's **coat of arms**.

According to the legend, a mermaid, called a *syrenka* in Polish, swam south from the Baltic Sea, down the Vistula River, to Warsaw where she freed fish from fishing nets. The fishermen were angry at first, but then were charmed by her singing. Later, a man captured the mermaid, planning to show her off to the public to make money. However, the Warsaw fishermen freed her. She was so grateful she promised to protect the city and its fishermen. A statue of the mermaid protector still stands in the Old Town section of Warsaw today.

PLINY'S SCALY MERMAIDS

Roman Pliny the Elder (23 CE–79 CE) wrote an encyclopedia of science called *Natural History* that people studied for centuries. He wrote of mermaids, which he called nereids: "And as for the Mermaids called Nereides, it is no fabulous [mythical] tale . . . how painters draw them, so they are indeed: only their body is rough and scaled all over, even in those parts where they resemble a woman."

Warsaw, the capital city of Poland, still honors the legend of their mermaid protector, including with this statue.

IT'S A FACT!

In 2009, Kiryat Yam, a town in Israel, offered $1 million for a photograph of a mermaid spotted off the coast!

Columbus Saw What?

You likely have heard about Christopher Columbus landing in the Americas in 1492, but you might not know he claimed he saw mermaids near today's Dominican Republic in 1493. They weren't the attractive creatures he had seen in pictures. He said they were "not half as beautiful as they are painted."

Some people think the mermaids Columbus and other sailors saw may have been manatees. Manatees live in warm waters of the Atlantic Ocean, waters through which Columbus traveled. Manatees are gray, brown, or black with bodies that narrow into a flat tail. They have flippers too. Florida manatees can grow to be more than 10 feet (3 m) in length. When these creatures came up for air, could Columbus and his crew have mistaken them for mermaids?

DUGONGS

Dugongs (at right, top) are related to manatees. They often travel alone or in pairs, though they've been spotted in large herds. They live in the Indian and Pacific Oceans, so they couldn't have been in Columbus's path through the Atlantic Ocean and Caribbean Sea. Steller's sea cow (at right, bottom) was in the same family as the dugong, but it was much larger. It lived in colder, Arctic waters, but was hunted to extinction in the 1700s.

Sailors may have mistaken manatees for mermaids because they were unfamiliar with marine life in warm climates.

IT'S A FACT!

Steller's sea cows, manatees, and dugongs are in a group of related animals called sirenians. This group was named after the sirens of Greek myth.

Henry Hudson's Crew Too

English explorer Henry Hudson is known for his North American travels. In 1608, on a trip north of Russia, he wrote about his crew seeing a mermaid in his journal. (Notice the different spelling of that time.)

This morning one of our companie [company] looking over boord saw a mermaid, and calling up some of the companie to see her, one more came up and by that time shee was come close to the ships side, looking earnestly on the men. . . . From the navill [navel] upward her backe [back] and breasts were like a womans, . . . but her body as big as one of us. Her skin very white, and long haire hanging downe behinde of colour blacke. In her going downe they saw her tayle [tail], which was like the tayle of a porposse [porpoise], and speckled like a macrell [mackerel].

CHECKING THE FACTS

Another often-told story said John Smith, leader of Virginia's Jamestown Colony, saw a mermaid in 1614. But people have had a hard time confirming this account. Smith wasn't in the West Indies, where he was supposed to have seen it, at that time. One scholar traced the tale to an 1849 newspaper article written by Alexandre Dumas, the author of the books *The Count of Monte Cristo* and *The Three Musketeers*.

Did Henry Hudson's crew really see a mermaid with white skin and black hair? Or could it have been a Steller's sea cow?

IT'S A FACT!

Henry Hudson reached Greenland and the East Coast of the United States in his travels in the early 1600s.

Some Explanations

Oceans cover about three-fourths of Earth. They haven't been fully explored yet, but so far, no proof of merfolk has been found. Today, most people accept that mermaids were the products of sailors' imaginations. But how could so many sailors have seen them?

Remember, a sailor long ago had to work hard day and night on a rocking ship for months (or sometimes years) at a time. Some ships weren't stocked with enough food and water to feed their crew. Without enough food, water, or sleep, people can **hallucinate**. And before electricity, it would have been hard to see much after the sun set. A long figure with a tail diving beneath the surface of the water, like a manatee, could easily be mistaken for a mermaid in the dark.

WHAT IF?

An oceanographer named Karl Banse wrote an article in 1990 about what mermaids might have been like if they were real. It was called "Mermaids: Their Biology, Culture, and Demise." Banse said mermaids would have lived in warm water since they didn't have blubber, a kind of fat, to survive in cold water. He also said they went extinct after being killed off by jellyfish stings. While Banse was joking, he applied real marine biology concepts to his ideas.

With nothing to look at for days in hard conditions, could sailors have imagined merfolk?

Possible Explanations for Merfolk Sightings

- Manatees, dugongs, seals, or other sea animals were mistaken for merfolk.
- Travelers had hallucinations from lack of food, water, or sleep on sea voyages.
- A lack of light caused sailors to mistake an animal or wave for merfolk.
- Stories passed down from mermaid folklore were accepted as fact.
- Mermaid hoaxes or jokes were accepted as fact.
- Merfolk are real.

IT'S A FACT!

The pouch that protects a developing baby shark or skate, a kind of ray, is called a mermaid's purse!

"The Little Mermaid"

"The Little Mermaid" is among the most famous mermaid tales. In the fairy tale, a mermaid falls in love with a human prince and gives up her underwater life to be with him. A sea witch takes the mermaid's beautiful voice in exchange for helping her grow legs. The mermaid becomes able to walk on land, but every step is painful. The sea witch warns her that if she doesn't win the love of the prince, she will die and become a wave in the ocean.

Sadly, the prince falls in love with someone else. The Little Mermaid, heartbroken, is given another chance to live and return to her underwater life—if she kills the prince. She refuses. Because of her virtue, she becomes a spirit, doing good deeds until she can enter heaven.

DISNEY'S *THE LITTLE MERMAID*

The story "The Little Mermaid" became a Disney movie of the same name in 1989, but it was much different. Scary, violent parts of Hans Christian Andersen's fairy tale were softened for young viewers. The Little Mermaid, who was given the name Ariel, gets her voice back and has a happy ending with her prince. Check out the Venn diagram on the next page to see key similarities and differences between the story and the movie.

Danish author Hans Christian Andersen wrote "The Little Mermaid" in 1836. This statue of the character is in Copenhagen, Denmark.

IT'S A FACT!

Hans Christian Andersen wrote other famous fairy tales, including "The Princess and the Pea," "The Ugly Duckling," and "The Emperor's New Clothes."

Comparing the Little Mermaid in the Fairy Tale and Disney Movie

Fairy Tale

- she doesn't have a name
- she has a grandmother
- she is in pain when she walks
- she doesn't win the prince's love
- she becomes a spirit at the tale's end

Both

- she saves a human prince's life and falls in love with him
- she wants to be human
- she trades her voice to a sea witch for legs

Movie

- her name is Ariel
- she has animal friends
- she isn't in pain when she walks
- she wins the prince's love
- she becomes a princess at the tale's end

The Famous Feejee Mermaid

In 1842, circus showman P. T. Barnum began displaying the body of a mermaid in his New York City museum. Although this mermaid, called the Feejee (or Fiji) Mermaid, had already been declared a fake in England, Barnum cleverly hooked the public by planting fake letters about it in newspapers. He hired a man to pretend to be a scientist who included the mermaid in an amazing animal collection. "Dr. Griffin" also exhibited another strange but real creature that had recently been discovered—a platypus.

Griffin pretended he would only allow the public to view the Feejee Mermaid for a short time. People flocked to see it while they could, for a fee. They didn't seem to mind that it didn't look like the beautiful creatures in the newspaper ads for the exhibit.

THE TRAVELING MERMAID

A Japanese fisherman may have created the Feejee Mermaid in the early 1800s. A Dutch merchant then purchased it and sold it to an American captain named Samuel Barrett Eades for $6,000. Eades may have believed it really was a mermaid. He gave the creature to his son, who sold it to the owner of a museum in Boston, Massachusetts. This owner, Moses Kimball, worked with P. T. Barnum to interest the public in the Feejee Mermaid.

The Feejee Mermaid was created by sewing together the top half of an ape and a fish tail. This startling creature wasn't the only hoax mermaid created this way.

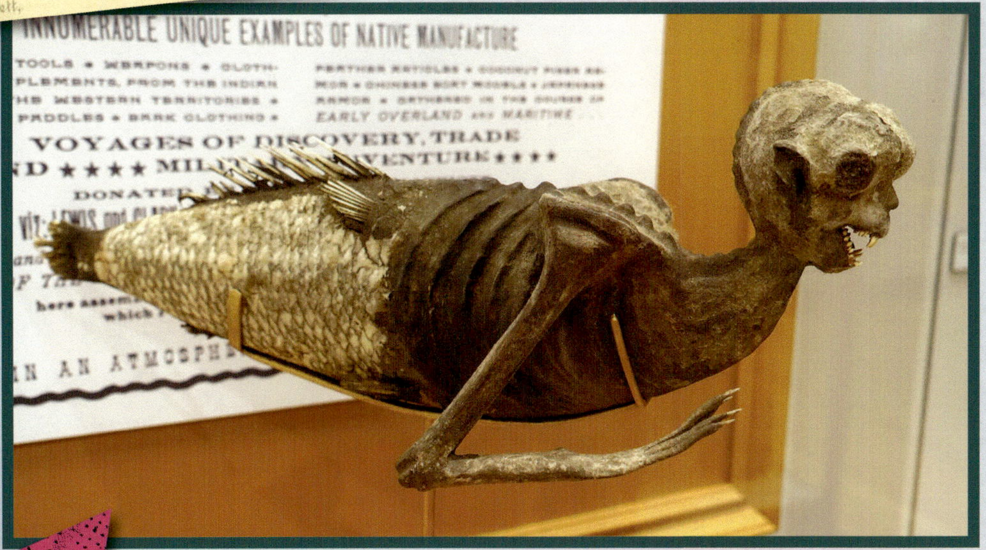

IT'S A FACT!

The Feejee Mermaid might have later burned in a fire, but no one is sure what happened to it. Harvard University's Peabody Museum has a hoax mermaid on display from around that time.

Modern "Mermaids"

Coney Island in New York City hosts a Mermaid Parade every year. People dress up like mermaids and other creatures to celebrate the beginning of summer. It's a way for artists to show off their creativity with costumes and other art forms.

In China, mermaid diving has become a popular sport. These **free divers** don't use tanks to breathe underwater; they hold their breath. Their legs are paired within a mermaid tail, so they must learn to swim with their stomach muscles, bending at the waist, much like a mermaid might. As of 2021, more than 1,000 instructors in China are teaching people about mermaid diving.

Some schools in the United States and Canada teach people to swim with a mermaid tail too. You can even buy or make your own tail!

THE MERMAID RECORD

In 2021, swimmers in China set the Guinness World Record for largest underwater mermaid show. The group—110 pro mermaid swimmers—performed in a tank at the Atlantis Sanya resort in Sanya, Hainan, China. In addition to swimming with their mermaid tails, the swimmers did spins, held hands, and performed other challenging movements. Around 90 percent of these performers were mermaid diving instructors.

The first Coney Island Mermaid Parade took place in 1983.

IT'S A FACT!

Coney Island has a street called Mermaid Avenue!

What Do You Believe?

While it's hard to catch a glimpse of actual mermaids and mermen, they're certainly a part of modern life. They're depicted in art, films, television shows, and books. You probably see them in ads too. Something about them and the idea of living underwater still interests people, thousands of years after the first merfolk myths. But are these creatures real?

Some people think it's possible that some sort of merpeople could have **evolved** from apes that lived near or even in water. This is called the aquatic ape theory. If this were true, could merfolk still be alive, perhaps hiding in a part of the ocean that hasn't been explored yet? It's time to decide what you believe about mermaids!

WHAT NOAA SAID

The U.S. National Oceanic and Atmospheric Administration (NOAA) weighed in on the mermaid question in 2012. A TV show called *Mermaids: The Body Found* aired on the Discovery Channel and Animal Planet. It was shot like a **documentary** and seemed to show the body of a mermaid. People who watched the show thought it was convincing and asked NOAA about its truthfulness. NOAA responded on its website, "No evidence of aquatic humanoids has ever been found."

The tails that professional mermaid performers wear can weigh up to 40 pounds (18 kg)!

IT'S A FACT!

A mummified shark was mistaken for the dead body of a mermaid. According to folklore, it was hung to help guard an Austrian city.

Glossary

Aboriginal: having to do with Australia's Native Peoples

coat of arms: a design of symbols standing for a family, city, or country

documentary: a movie or TV program presenting information about an issue

enchanted: being held in the power of a magic spell

epic: a long form of poetry that tells the story of a legendary or historical hero

evolve: to grow and change over time

free diver: one who takes part in swimming underwater, often to great depth, with a mask and flippers but without portable breathing equipment

hallucinate: to hear, see, or sense in other ways someone or something that is not there

hypnotize: to put someone into a state that is like sleep but in which one hears and responds to a person's suggestions

mollusk: an animal that lacks a backbone and has a soft body, such as a snail, clam, or octopus

Norse: relating to ancient Norway

Scandinavian: from the region of northern Europe called Scandinavia now occupied by Norway, Sweden, and Denmark. Sometimes Scandinavia also includes Iceland and Finland.

technology: using science, engineering, and other industries to invent useful tools or to solve problems. Also a machine, piece of equipment, or method created by technology.

For More Information

Books

Alberti, Theresa Jarosz. *Mermaids*. New York, NY: AV2 by Weigl, 2020.

Andersen, Hans Christian. *The Little Mermaid*. New York, NY: NorthSouth, 2020.

Williams, Heather DiLorenzo. *Mermaid*. Fremont, CA: Full Tilt Press, 2022.

Websites

Are Mermaids Real?

oceanservice.noaa.gov/facts/mermaids.html

Read NOAA's answer to this question and explore ocean facts.

Mermaid

kids.britannica.com/kids/article/mermaid/399544

Learn more facts about mermaid folklore here!

How Mermaids Work

science.howstuffworks.com/science-vs-myth/strange-creatures/mermaids.htm

Read this overview of mermaids, both in myth and eyewitness accounts.

Publisher's note to educators and parents: Our editors have carefully reviewd these websites to ensure that they are suitable for students. Many websites change frequently, however, and we cannot guarantee that a site's future contents will continue to meet or high standardsof quality and educational value. Be advised that students should be closely supervised whenever they access the internet.

Index